DEVELOPING CREATIVITY

USING A CREATIVE APPROACH

WORKING WITH OTHERS

INTRODUCTION

The ability to think creatively is an essential skill for every manager. By applying your creativity, it is possible to break out of your usual routines and patterns of behavior and to increase your personal effectiveness. Thinking Creatively will show you how to tap into your innate creativity so that you can find innovative solutions to difficult problems. It will help you understand the process of generating and assessing ideas, and it will show you how to benefit from sharing ideas with others in order to build consensus and commitment. There are 101 tips throughout the book to give you practical advice, and self-assessment exercises enable you to evaluate your ability as a creative thinker. As you develop the techniques that will help you stimulate creativity in yourself and in others, you will find this book an invaluable guide.

UNDERSTANDING CREATIVITY

Thinking creatively helps you find ways to deal with challenges and form opportunities. Understand how creativity can help you become more successful in all areas of your life.

WHAT IS CREATIVITY?

Creativity is the process of challenging accepted ideas and ways of doing things in order to find new solutions or concepts. Be aware of the obstacles that stand in the way of the creative impulse and understand the benefits that creative thinking can bring you.

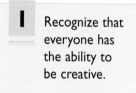

1 Recognize that everyone has the ability to be creative.

POINTS TO REMEMBER

- Our traditional approach to solving problems relies on logical, tried-and-tested methods.
- We can change our behavior patterns only by looking at issues from different angles.
- Creative thinking involves changing your assumptions and beliefs.
- Creativity does not always produce better solutions, but it helps you generate more ideas and offers you new insights.

DEFINING CREATIVITY

Being creative means seeing ideas or objects in a different context, either by recognizing their inherent potential to be used in a different way or by putting previously unconnected ideas together to create something completely new. All of us have the ability to be creative. However, we tend to be constrained by culture and circumstances and so do things the way we have always done them. Instead of seeing problems as opportunities to find new ways of doing things, we tend to see them as "hurdles" to be jumped. Use creative thinking to gain a new perspective on the world.

CREATIVE THINKING

Some people are naturally creative, but most of us accept things as they are. For example, a plastic bottle is only a bottle to some people. But to a creative thinker, it could also be a disposable container, a funnel, or a tiny greenhouse. Creative thinking starts with questioning. Are objects really just what we assume them to be? Or are they that way only because we see them like that?

◄ **BEING INVENTIVE**
We all instinctively use creative thinking to cope with daily situations, such as being caught in the rain. Learn to tap into your creativity at work, too.

BENEFITING FROM CREATIVITY

Over the centuries, creative people have provided new solutions to the problems of their day. The ability of human beings to find creative solutions to problems is essential for the well-being of the human race. On a social level, collective creativity provides the opportunity to improve quality of life. In organizations, creativity is essential to ensure a company's ongoing effectiveness in a changing world. On a personal level, creativity can help you break out of routines you dislike.

2 Change your current patterns of thinking.

3 Remember that change begins with questioning.

USING YOUR CREATIVITY

Take an everyday object, such as a paperclip. Ask yourself, "What can this be used for?" If your answer is "a paperclip," then you are responding "traditionally." If, however, you see it not only as a paperclip, but also as a piece of wire, then you are thinking creatively. From this perception, you will start to see that the paperclip has many uses. For example, it could be a fuse wire for an electric circuit, a marking instrument, or a clip for securing a box. Start noticing the potential in everything.

LOOKING AT OBJECTS ►
When you look at an ordinary object such as a paperclip, think about the different uses it could have.

USING LOGICAL AND CREATIVE THINKING

We generate ideas by thinking creatively, and then we use logical thinking to help turn these thoughts into realistic actions. Understand the benefits of both logical and creative thinking, so that you can start to adapt the way you think.

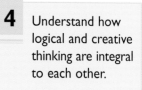

4 Understand how logical and creative thinking are integral to each other.

5 Use your past experiences to find solutions.

6 Think creatively to increase your opportunities.

THINKING LOGICALLY

When we are faced with a familiar problem, logical thinking enables us to tap into our personal experiences and find a suitable solution with the minimum of effort. By assessing a situation against your relevant experience, you can choose the most appropriate path, and move toward a solution. This logical approach, also known as convergent thinking, is very efficient. However, it can become a barrier when you have little relevant experience, when there are a few potential solutions, or when you need a brand new solution.

CASE STUDY

John was a relatively inexperienced mechanic. During the course of his work, he regularly had to repair old cars that had problems starting. In his experience, the fault would usually be a flat battery or a damp spark plug. If he found that these were working, he would then deduce that there was a problem with the starter. Using logical thinking allowed him to get to the root of problems quickly.

As his experience increased, his boss allowed him to start working on newer cars. He found that it was harder to pinpoint the starting problems on the more modern cars, because they had more elaborate systems. Instead of relying on his past experiences, he started to ask the car owners for details about the problems they were experiencing. He relied on his creativity to help him find the root of the problems.

◀ **ADAPTING YOUR THINKING**
In this example, a mechanic has learned to deal with common problems in a logical way, using his past experiences to guide him to solutions. However, he is then faced with situations where he lacks experience, and he has to start thinking more creatively.

THINKING CREATIVELY

Divergent thinking, or creative thinking, involves opening up your mind to find new solutions and new ways of doing things. Instead of taking your usual, logical approach to problem-solving, learn to suspend your judgment. When you are faced with a problem, start to look for different, more inventive solutions. Once you have generated as many ideas as possible, use a logical thinking process to refine your ideas and identify the best solution.

7 Explore possible options before making decisions.

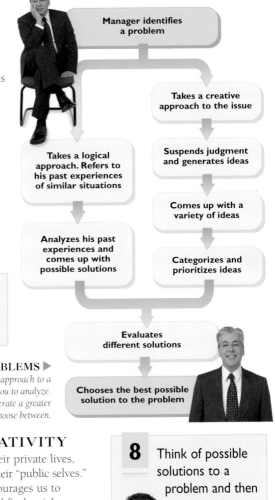

Manager identifies a problem

Takes a creative approach to the issue

Takes a logical approach. Refers to his past experiences of similar situations

Suspends judgment and generates ideas

Comes up with a variety of ideas

Analyzes his past experiences and comes up with possible solutions

Categorizes and prioritizes ideas

Evaluates different solutions

Chooses the best possible solution to the problem

SOLVING PROBLEMS ▶

Using either a logical or creative approach to a problem will produce solutions for you to analyze. However, creative thinking will generate a greater number of ideas to choose between.

EXPLORING CREATIVITY

Most people are creative in their private lives, but tend to be less creative in their "public selves." Our conditioned behavior encourages us to keep problems to ourselves and find quick fixes that involve as few people as possible. Start to break this habit. When you are faced with a problem, spend time exploring ideas, and involve other people in your search for solutions.

8 Think of possible solutions to a problem and then evaluate them using logical thinking.

BECOMING CREATIVE

We all have the ability to be creative, but this mind-set is better developed in some people than in others. Examine how to overcome the conditioning that blocks your creativity, and learn to use your knowledge and experience more productively.

9 Use your imagination to find different solutions.

UNLOCKING CREATIVITY

We are brought up to believe that certain behaviors and thoughts are "right" and others are "wrong." This conditioning constrains our thinking and prevents us from finding new answers. Unlock your creativity. Empower yourself to question your ways of doing things.

Connects the unconnected

Generates new solutions

Remains open-minded

Challenges old ideas

Uses imagination

Asks questions

THINKING CREATIVELY ▶
The person who is able to work outside the bounds of his or her experience and seek new solutions to problems will be more successful in the long run.

IDENTIFYING TYPES OF CONDITIONING

TYPE	POINTS TO NOTE
SOCIAL	This type of conditioning equips us to fit into the society in which we live. However, it discourages us from challenging the status quo.
LEARNING	We are taught to learn in a structured way. However, this means that we have a tendency to accept facts rather than challenging them.
FAMILY	Parental authority lays down our patterns and rules of behavior at an early age – these become instinctive and are hard to break.
WORKPLACE	This conditioning sets the rules for behavior at work. We have a tendency to accept procedures as they are and not to question those in authority.

THINGS TO DO

1. Identify something that you would like to change.

2. Think of the change you would like and identify what is holding you back.

3. Decide what action you could take, and then take it.

LOOKING AT INFORMATION

Our minds store vast amounts of information. When you receive an input signal, such as someone asking you a question, your mind will automatically access its relevant data store. Without this natural ability, you would spend a lot of time doing ordinary things. For example, finding your way to work would be a new experience every day. However, this mental process, which makes us very efficient in our everyday lives, is a barrier to creativity. Avoid making instant assumptions and connections.

11 Aim to look at information in more productive, insightful ways.

THINKING DIFFERENTLY

We are conditioned not to think the unthinkable. For example, many people prefer not to ask for an explanation about an issue they do not understand, for fear of looking stupid. Let go of preconceived ideas and break the glass wall of conditioning in order to find your creative self. Avoid accepting procedures as they are, just because they have always been that way. Seek ways of doing things differently and always aim to increase your effectiveness and that of your organization.

10 Understand how conditioning forces you to think in a prescribed way and limits your potential.

THE CREATIVE PROCESS

Look at the diagram below. Where would the letter "F" go in the following sequence? Do you imagine that it will go above or below the line?:

A   E
_____
    B   C   D

There is in fact no obvious "right" answer. The "F" could go beside the "E" as part of a 1/3/2 sequence. Or it could go below the line as part of a 1/3/1/3 sequence. Alternatively, it could go next to the "E" so that all the letters that are made up of straight lines are above the line. Some people will dismiss this problem as not solvable, while others will assume that only one answer can be right. A creative person accepts that whatever he or she wants to believe is right and that there are lots of possibilities.

UNDERSTANDING THE CREATIVE PROCESS

When you bring together ideas that were not previously connected or see new ways of doing things, you are thinking creatively. Examine how the creative process works and start to change your current patterns of thinking.

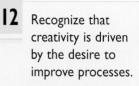

12 Recognize that creativity is driven by the desire to improve processes.

USING HUMOR

Humor provides an analogy to the creative process. The basic storyline of a joke is logical and usually depicts an everyday situation. As the listener, you recognize the scenario and think you know how the story will progress. The punch line then destroys your preconceptions. You are "jumped" from one store of information to another.

▲ PLAYING ON PEOPLE'S ASSUMPTIONS
When a comedian tells a joke, the listeners make assumptions about what will happen next in the story – the punch line destroys these assumptions in a way that makes people laugh.

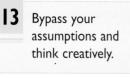

13 Bypass your assumptions and think creatively.

14 Believe that you can think of solutions.

DOS AND DON'TS

✔ Do be open-minded in your approach to situations and people.

✔ Do be ready to adapt your attitude to suit different occasions.

✔ Do break out of the box of past experience.

✘ Don't assume that what was right for yesterday is automatically right for today, too.

✘ Don't be misled by your preconceptions.

✘ Don't just take the path of least resistance.

BREAKING PATTERNS

Learn to override your natural thinking processes and your tendency to rely on your usual way of doing things, so that you can find new solutions. Identify how you would normally deal with a difficult situation, and then deliberately adopt a different approach. For example, perhaps you are faced with a seemingly impossible deadline. Instead of deciding to work late to make sure that the work is finished on time, think about what would happen if the schedule were amended. Notice how changing your approach creates new opportunities.

15 Try not to be constrained by rules.

16 Accept that problems are the food of creativity.

CHANGING ▶ YOUR APPROACH
In this example, a manager always felt anxious before negotiations – she disliked the feeling of confrontation. However, she learned how to break this cycle by visualizing what she wanted to achieve from negotiations and by changing the way she viewed her customer relationships.

CASE STUDY

Joanna was a sales manager for a software company. She was good at her job, but she tended to get anxious about face-to-face negotiations.

She spoke to her boss about this, and he suggested that instead of looking at negotiations as potential confrontations, she should try to focus on them as opportunities to develop customer relationships and to meet mutual needs.

The next time Joanna was preparing for a negotiation, she began to visualize what she wanted to achieve from the discussion, and what the other party would want to gain, too.

By approaching the situation from a new angle, she began to think of new possibilities that both parties could benefit from. She thought about how she could work in a collaborative way with the customer, and she began to look forward to meetings.

POINTS TO REMEMBER

- Imagination can free you from the chains of past experience.
- You need to use your imagination to ensure that you have the future you desire, not the future someone else has planned.
- Your imagination can help you to project yourself into "fantasy" situations. Then you can start making your dreams become achievable reality.

USING YOUR IMAGINATION

All creative thinking techniques work on the basis of imposing a condition on your thinking; for example, they encourage the use of your imagination. Imagination is the lifeblood of creativity. Use it to disrupt your natural thinking patterns. For example, when you are unsure about what you want from your job, visualize your desired future. Create a vision that you can work toward. Then, use your logical mind to work out how you can make this goal a reality.

IDENTIFYING THINKING PATTERNS

In order to become more creative, you need to be aware of how you usually respond to situations or issues. Notice your current behavior patterns and ways of thinking and test how creative you really are – be honest with yourself.

> **17** Understand your thinking processes so that you are able to adapt them.

QUESTIONS TO ASK YOURSELF

Q If someone suggests a new way of doing something, do I embrace it or do I feel anxious about making changes?

Q Do I tend to stick to routines, or am I willing to be flexible?

Q Am I judgmental toward other people?

Q Am I able to see the whole problem or do I get caught up in the finer details?

UNDERSTANDING THE WAY YOU THINK

It is hard to generalize about people's thinking processes, because individuals tend to react to different situations in different ways. For example, a manager may find that he or she works in a very structured way at work, but is chaotic at home. Notice how you react to certain scenarios, so that you can start to change the way you think. Ask yourself searching questions. What do you think obstructs your creative impulses? For example, do you find that you are always so busy that you never make time to think creatively?

ANALYZING YOUR ▶
BEHAVIOR PATTERNS
This manager always tries to cope with his workload instead of finding creative ways to work more efficiently.

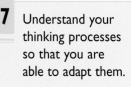

Manager struggles to deal with various tasks at once

ASSESSING YOUR CREATIVE POTENTIAL

The following statements are designed to provide you with some insight into your current level of creativity. On a piece of paper, make a note of your responses to each question (a, b, or c) and then assess your results.

1. You have been invited to join some friends for a ski trip. Do you:
a) Worry about who will look after things while you are away.
b) Doubt that you will have the time.
c) Accept it as a marvelous opportunity.

2. You are faced with a recurring problem at work. Do you:
a) Draw it to your manager's attention.
b) Immediately try to solve it yourself.
c) Call a meeting with all involved.

3. You arrive home to find that the dog has destroyed your new shoes. Do you:
a) Blame yourself.
b) Punish the dog.
c) Go and buy a new pair of shoes.

4. You are on vacation and discover that the return flight is delayed. Do you:
a) Call work and say you will be back late.
b) Sit at the airport and wait.
c) Enjoy the extension of your vacation.

5. Part of your yard is very overgrown. Do you:
a) Clear it yourself.
b) Hire somebody else to do the work.
c) Make a fun day of it with friends.

6. You are concerned about passing an exam. Do you:
a) Study hard.
b) Talk to someone who has already taken the exam and develop a study plan.
c) Organize private coaching with a tutor.

7. Your children are bored. Do you:
a) Promise to buy them some new toys.
b) Play with them.
c) Help them to find something they want to do and teach them how to do it.

8. You have a difficult relationship with a relative. Do you:
a) Pretend that there isn't a problem.
b) Try to minimize contact.
c) Find a common interest and build on it.

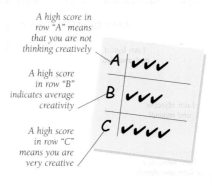

A high score in row "A" means that you are not thinking creatively

A high score in row "B" indicates average creativity

A high score in row "C" means you are very creative

UNDERSTANDING YOUR THOUGHT PROCESSES

Research indicates that the two hemispheres of the brain process information in different ways, and your natural thinking style will depend on the side of your brain you tend to be led by. Decide whether you are naturally creative.

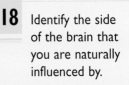

18 Identify the side of the brain that you are naturally influenced by.

POINTS TO REMEMBER

- We use both sides of our brain for successful creative thinking.
- We use the right side of our brain for creating ideas and the left side for analyzing them.
- Logical thinkers can develop their creative potential.

THINKING PATTERNS ▼
Organized people are more influenced by the left side of the brain, while intuitive people are influenced by the right side.

UNDERSTANDING HOW YOUR BRAIN WORKS

The left part of the brain processes information in a logical way, while the right part of your brain focuses on the creative, intuitive, part of your personality. Most people tend to be dominated by one or other side of their brains and have a distinct thinking style. Some people can adapt to both modes. People who are dominated by the right side of their brains are naturally creative but this does not mean that people who are dominated by the left side of their brains cannot be creative.

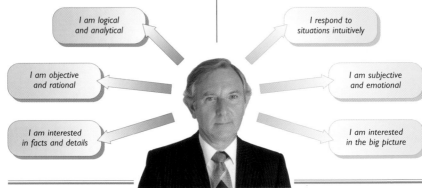

LEFT-BRAINED PERSON | RIGHT-BRAINED PERSON

I am logical and analytical

I respond to situations intuitively

I am objective and rational

I am subjective and emotional

I am interested in facts and details

I am interested in the big picture

Logical thinker plans week's work

RECOGNIZING LEFT-BRAIN DOMINANCE

The left side of the brain processes information by taking small, separate pieces and building up a "big" picture from which it draws conclusions. Individuals who are more influenced by the left hemisphere of the brain work through problems logically. They are good at developing strategies and like to base their decisions on facts. They are articulate, good communicators. While they tend to conform to rules, they are also adaptable.

▲ BEING ORGANIZED
Left-brained people tend to work in a structured, routine-driven way. They tend to plan their daily schedules, and work through lists of tasks in a methodical, ordered way.

19 Notice how you approach problems, and think about whether you are naturally creative.

RECOGNIZING RIGHT-BRAIN DOMINANCE

People who are dominated by the right side of their brains are not happy to just follow an instruction and complete a task. They need to know why they are doing it. These people like to see, hear, and feel, what is required of them. They trust their feelings and answer questions intuitively. Notice whether you tend to think in this way or not. Even if you are not naturally creative, you can learn how to change your approach.

Manager discusses all the options with her team before making decisions

NATURALLY CREATIVE ▶
People who are dominated by the right side of their brains like to find out the full picture before they start a project.

ASSESSING YOUR NATURAL CREATIVITY

Evaluate whether you are more influenced by the creative right side of your brain or the logical left side of your brain. Read the following statements and indicate whether you agree or disagree with them. Be as honest as you can. Check the analysis below to see how you scored. Use your answers to identify how you could change your thinking processes and become more creative.

OPTIONS

A Agree

B Disagree

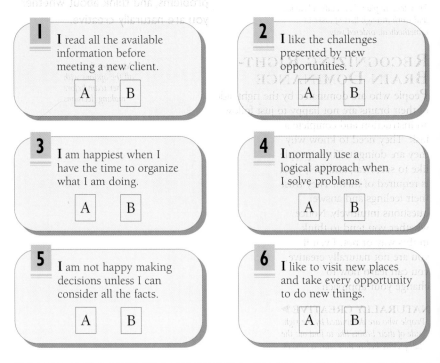

1 I read all the available information before meeting a new client.

A   B

2 I like the challenges presented by new opportunities.

A   B

3 I am happiest when I have the time to organize what I am doing.

A   B

4 I normally use a logical approach when I solve problems.

A   B

5 I am not happy making decisions unless I can consider all the facts.

A   B

6 I like to visit new places and take every opportunity to do new things.

A   B

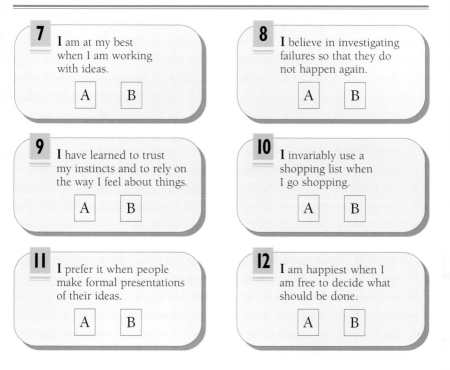

7 I am at my best when I am working with ideas.

A B

8 I believe in investigating failures so that they do not happen again.

A B

9 I have learned to trust my instincts and to rely on the way I feel about things.

A B

10 I invariably use a shopping list when I go shopping.

A B

11 I prefer it when people make formal presentations of their ideas.

A B

12 I am happiest when I am free to decide what should be done.

A B

ANALYSIS

Check your results against the following to see whether you are dominated by the right- or left-hand side of your brain:

1/ A=left, B=right 2/ A=right, B=left
3/ A=left, B=right 4/ A=left, B=right
5/ A=left, B=right 6/ A=right, B=left
7/ A=right, B=left 8/ A=left, B=right
9/ A=right, B=left 10/ A=left, B=right
11/ A=left, B=right 12/ A=right, B=left

If most of your answers were "left," this indicates that you are a left-brain thinker.

You like structure and logic and should concentrate on thinking more creatively. A near equal score suggests a balance between logical and creative thinking. If your score has a high percentage of "right," you are a right-brain thinker and are naturally creative. But remember, there is always room for improvement.

DEVELOPING CREATIVITY

In order to succeed in developing your innate creativity, you need to overcome the natural barriers in your mind. Start to challenge your usual approach to situations.

OVERCOMING BARRIERS

A big barrier to creative thinking is a tendency to seek quick solutions to problems. This may help you in the short term, but you will not excel in the long run. Look at the way you currently use your time, and start to spend more time being creative.

20 Recognize the advantages and pitfalls of different thinking patterns.

21 Structure your time so that it is more productive.

22 Generate lots of ideas before making decisions.

ADAPTING YOUR THINKING PROCESSES

Human beings have a natural tendency to seek quick and simple solutions to problems. We often know the answer we want and make sure the facts support our chosen solution. However, some situations require a different, more creative approach. Divergent thinking focuses on generating as many ideas as possible and opening up new opportunities in order to find a "best fit" solution. Make the time to think creatively, think about the big picture, and don't rush to quick conclusions.

MAKING THE TIME

The Japanese believe that there are four types of managerial time: "operational time" – the time necessary to correct yesterday's errors; "strategic time" – the time needed to plan for the future; "innovative time" – the time needed to become more competitive tomorrow; and "kaizen time" – the time needed for the continuous improvements that ensure that we will have a tomorrow. It is generally true that we do not devote enough time to finding better ways of doing things. Make the time to review what you could improve in your work and your life, and then take action.

▲ SCHEDULING WORK
Review your schedules and delegate work to your team, so that you have time to focus on long-term goals.

TIME ANALYSIS

Look at how you currently spend your time and highlight areas where you could improve. First, keep a record of what you do during a typical week. Divide your time into four categories: operational (project work); strategic (planning for the future); innovative (seeking new approaches); kaizen (making ongoing improvements). Then, review your findings. You will probably find that you spend a significant amount of time on operational issues. Aim to increase your creative time: identify the operational activities you could reduce in order to allow you to do this. For example, you could delegate more of your work.

THINGS TO DO

1. Look at how you could increase the time you spend creatively.
2. Review procedures and think about how they could be improved.
3. Take time out to find creative solutions.

MANAGING YOUR TIME

The Japanese believe that senior managers should spend no more than 25 percent of their time on operational issues. The rest of their time should be spread across the other three categories. The more time senior managers spend on operational issues, the less time they can spend working creatively, and this reflects poor planning. Assess how you can restructure your time more effectively. Remember that the only way to manage time successfully is to set yourself realistic schedules, and then to stick to them.

BELIEVING IN CHANGE

We need to believe that we can think the unthinkable and believe the unbelievable. Challenge the accepted way of doing things. Overcome your fear of looking foolish in front of other people and have the courage to put forward your ideas.

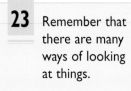

23 Remember that there are many ways of looking at things.

24 Be ready to question the accepted.

25 View problems as an impetus to change.

THINKING THE UNTHINKABLE

New ideas are essential for progress, yet most new ideas are initially perceived in a negative way. The unknown is seen as dangerous, and an individual's instinctive response to a new idea is often to reject it, because it is safer to stay with what he or she has already tried and tested. Have the courage to think the unthinkable. Persuade others that what seem like impossible ideas are possible.

CHALLENGING BELIEFS

Sometimes we have creative ideas, but we are reluctant to put them forward because they may create precedents that "go outside the box" of accepted beliefs. You may not like to say something that others may find challenging and thus reject. Being creative means not only having the ability to come up with ideas but also being willing to challenge the conventional wisdom. Realize that all creative solutions, by their very nature, involve change and change involves having the courage to challenge the status quo.

▲ **CONSIDERING THE IMPOSSIBLE**
In the past, few people believed that sending a man to the Moon would ever be possible. However, it became a reality because people had the courage to believe in it and make it happen.

BENEFITING FROM CHANGE

People are intuitively opposed to any idea that they see as "not being in their best interest." The problem is that one person opposing a new idea does not stop others from benefiting from it. For example, deciding not to implement a technical innovation in your organization does not prevent a competitor from making that change. Recognize that those who fail to change will be left behind.

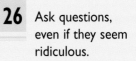

26 Ask questions, even if they seem ridiculous.

▼ **ACCEPTING CHANGE**
Change occurs when people recognize the potential advantages an idea can bring and work to put it into action.

Listen to ideas with an open mind	Accept that change is necessary	Implement creative solutions

POINTS TO REMEMBER

● Close-ended problems have one solution. For example, a flat battery will need to be replaced.

● Open-ended problems are those that have many possible answers, such as planning an office layout.

● A great barrier to creativity is the fear of looking foolish.

TAKING A NEW APPROACH

Being creative means using a different approach to the way you solve certain problems. This is not something you need to do all the time – this approach is time-consuming and irrelevant when the solution to the problem is clear (close-ended). However, if a problem is open-ended and has a number of potential solutions, start to form some creative ideas and discuss them with others.

IGNORING RIDICULE

When you put forward a creative idea, you stand the risk of being called foolish. No one wants to look foolish in front of their peers and this innate fear often prevents people from voicing their ideas. Do not be deterred by the fear of being ridiculed – have confidence in yourself when you express your ideas.

RISKING RIDICULE ▶
This assistant is sharing an idea with his team. He does not let their ridicule deter him from explaining the idea.

Colleague laughs at assistant's idea

Assistant presents an abstract idea

Manager listens attentively

CHANGING YOUR APPROACH

To be able to increase your inventiveness, you need to learn how to tap into your mind's creative resources. Practice changing your natural approach to problems until the new method becomes instinctive. Take the time to exercise your mind.

27 Recognize that developing creativity takes time and practice.

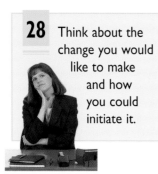

28 Think about the change you would like to make and how you could initiate it.

PREPARING TO CHANGE

The way you do things is determined by your values – your beliefs. These are influenced by the culture you grew up in and they are also affected by your character. Thus, if you enjoy structure, you will tend to resist changes that appear to cut across your desire for order. If you prefer a flexible lifestyle, you will resist changes that threaten to impose order on you. Recognize that adapting your behavior requires practice, until the change in your approach becomes a "natural" impulse.

LEARNING TO CHANGE

Change is one of the few constants in life. Some people fight it, some embrace it, others "wait and see." But no one can avoid it. Try following a set process to move from a current behavior to a new one. For example, for some people, being overweight is a lifestyle problem. Changing this situation means following guidelines (a diet) and having regular weight checks (feedback) to create new eating habits. Identify the change you want to make, commit to the change, resolve any potential obstacles in your path, and then take action.

MAKING CHANGES ▶

It is useful to follow a structured process to help you create a change in a behavior pattern. Take a step-by-step approach and ask a friend to give you regular feedback on your progress.

RECOGNITION
Understand the reason for making a change

DECISION
Be committed to making the change

PERMISSION
Gain consent from other parties involved

ACTION
Take the necessary action to make the change

EXERCISING YOUR MIND

Developing your creative potential means freeing up your mind. Just as someone who is used to a sedentary lifestyle and decides to take a hiking vacation needs to get in shape before the trip, so you need to train your mind to work in new ways before you can develop your own creative potential. Try exercising your mind. For example, imagine where you would like to be in a year's time. Focus the image so that you can touch, hear, and feel it. Develop a plan that will help you achieve this goal.

29 Remove your self-imposed mental roadblocks by carrying out creative exercises.

▲ DOING EXERCISES
Carry out some simple exercises to stimulate your creative thinking and teach your mind to think in new ways.

PRACTICING DIFFERENT THINKING STYLES

THINKING STYLE	ACTIONS TO TAKE
CONSIDERING CONTEXTS	Think about something that you habitually do; for example, you always go on a beach vacation. Make a list of different vacation ideas. Then, think about what you are seeking from your usual vacation and see if any of the options satisfy this need in a way that you had not considered before.
SEEKING ALTERNATIVES	Choose an idea or object that you would like to explore. For example, think about a dry erase pen. How many different uses could it have? Make a list. Then, review your ideas to see if any of them provide another use that might be interesting.
MAKING CONNECTIONS	Choose a product or idea and see how many different situations you can connect it to. For example, think about the potential uses for a boat's sail. When you have exhausted your ideas, examine the connections to see what new insights they provide.

COACHING FOR CREATIVITY

Many organizations use coaching to help their staff acquire new skills or develop existing ones. Understand the coaching process, see how you can use it to improve your creative potential, and set yourself goals to work toward.

30 Use coaching to help you change your current thinking patterns.

31 Ask a colleague you admire for advice on how to improve your creative skills.

WHAT IS COACHING?

Coaching is a useful tool that can help you develop your strengths and improve your skills. There are a number of ways that coaching can be carried out: for example, through observation and feedback or through organized sessions with a personal coach. Coaching sessions, in which the coach provides leadership and a framework for generating creative ideas, is the most suitable method for developing creativity. The coach is able to support and guide the individual being coached (the coachee), and offer advice when necessary. By the end of the sessions, the coachee is also in a position to coach others.

FINDING A COACH

Coaches lead by example. Thus, to be an effective creative thinking coach, the individual must understand how creativity works in practice. He or she must also have a good knowledge of the various techniques that can help develop creative thinking. Find a suitable professional coach and set up a series of coaching sessions. Alternatively, ask a friend to act as your coach. Before you have the first session, think through what you want to achieve during the coaching process. For example, decide that you want to learn how to deal with problems in a more creative way.

32 Set a fixed amount of time for a coaching session.

33 Form clear goals to work toward during a coaching session.

Coach talks through
agreed upon
action steps

BEING COACHED

During the first session, the coach should take the lead. He or she may ask you questions about your normal thinking processes or your reactions to particular situations. Discussing these issues will help you pinpoint what you could start to do differently. Allow the coach to prompt you to make suggestions. Then, set yourself achievable weekly targets and draw up an action plan. Agree on how these will be monitored and set a date for the next coaching session.

▲ WORKING WITH A COACH
Take notes during the coaching session and put your set action plan in writing. Schedule a date by which these tasks will be achieved – discuss timings with your coach to make sure they are realistic.

COACHING TECHNIQUES

For coaching to succeed, make sure that you adhere to a structure during your coaching sessions. If necessary, divide your allotted time into sections. Spend the first five minutes discussing the problem you want to resolve. Spend the next 10 minutes identifying your goals. Move on to discussing possible solutions, before taking 10 minutes to write down your action plan. Always leave a coaching session on a high note, with concrete goals set out and scheduled.

34 Recognize that coaching is an effective means of changing your current patterns of behavior.

DOS AND DON'TS

✔ Do be open to suggestions and feedback.

✔ Do be realistic about the targets you set yourself.

✔ Do treat coaching as an investment in your personal development.

✔ Do set yourself small steps – then you can achieve each one with ease before moving on to the next one.

✘ Don't expect immediate results.

✘ Don't expect your coach to have all the answers.

✘ Don't use a coaching session as a chance to express your worries.

✘ Don't set yourself goals that you cannot monitor. Make sure that you and your coach can assess your achievements.

STIMULATING CREATIVE THINKING

There is a wide range of tools that you can use to stimulate creative thinking processes. They are simple to use and effective in practice. Familiarize yourself with the different creative tools and start to understand how you can apply them.

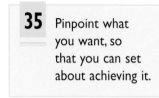

35 Pinpoint what you want, so that you can set about achieving it.

36 Think in terms of the results you want to achieve.

37 Focus on questions rather than predicting answers.

CLARIFYING THE OUTCOME

In many situations, your reaction to a problem is instinctive. You may not even think about what outcome you actually require, and the results you finally get are therefore not always what you want. A useful way to approach a problem is to define the outcome before you start the problem-solving journey and then apply your creativity to achieving it. In this way, you will have reference points against which to evaluate your ideas. For example, if your desired outcome is to gain a new customer, focus your creative energies on achieving that.

CASE STUDY

John was a manager for a supermarket. Stock deliveries took place three times a week, but it was difficult to deal with the number of trucks arriving at the store at the same time. Deliveries were causing congestion, the truck drivers were frustrated about delays, and the staff was having difficulties dealing with the influx of goods.
John saw that a solution could be to receive deliveries

five days a week – this would reduce congestion. However, he then saw that this would cause stock-control problems.
He realized that while he wanted to reduce congestion, he wanted to retain three delivery days. His solution was to create a loading times rotation schedule.
By clarifying what he wanted to achieve, John was able to resolve the problem without causing any unwanted or unforeseen changes.

◀ **DEFINING AN OUTCOME**
In this example, a manager was faced with a problem. Although an obvious solution sprang to mind, he realized that this proposal could cause other problems. He clarified his goals, and then he was able to work through to a creative solution.

USING PHYSICAL ACTIVITY

Certain types of physical activity can provide the right conditions for creative thinking. This is because, when you exercise, your motor senses are occupied with the basics of keeping your body functioning effectively. This frees the creative part of your mind to explore ideas. Choose a sport that you enjoy and make it a regular part of your routine – take advantage of the time to think.

▲ **BENEFITING FROM EXERCISE**
When your body is engaged in a repetitive physical activity, such as swimming or jogging, your mind is free to explore complex issues and come up with creative solutions.

38 Learn to cross the natural barriers in your mind.

USING MIND MAPPING

This process is designed to help you change the way you look at complex problems. When you are faced with a problem, impose it onto a "model" so that you view it in a different way. For example, draw the shape of a tree. Write down the main parts of the problem next to the large branches; note smaller aspects of the issue against the secondary branches, and so on. Once you have separated out the problem in this way, apply your creativity to each part of the issue, rather than trying to tackle the problem as an unwieldy whole.

Annotates tree with aspects of problem to be solved

Manager thinks about problem to be solved and breaks it into separate issues

◀ **BUILDING A PICTURE**
Mind mapping provides a logical frame for analyzing problems by separating problems into manageable parts.

USING THE "HELICOPTER" APPROACH

Most of our behavior is subconscious. We tend to react to people's body language automatically, rather than thinking about what that behavior means and responding accordingly. Adopt what is known as the "helicopter" approach. When you are talking to someone, consciously interpret his or her nonverbal behavior before responding. This will give you an insight into the other person's feelings and help you create better mutual understanding.

Colleague makes her point with strong feeling

Manager interprets colleague's nonverbal signals

He realizes that she feels strongly about issue

Manager shows understanding and situation is defused

Manager feels disconcerted by colleague's behavior

Manager takes offense at colleague's aggressive body language

USING A "HELICOPTER" ▲
In this example, a manager must consider what his colleague's brusque behavior signifies before he responds, so that he can build understanding between them. If he instinctively reacts in a negative way, their discussion will break down.

IMPOSING A CONDITION

When you impose an external condition on a problem, you change the way you look at it. For example, perhaps you want to buy a new house, but you have a budget problem. Instead of asking, "What can I get for my money?" ask, "How can I change my home without spending any money?" This might lead you to think of solutions you had not previously considered, such as remortgaging.

RECOGNIZING THE ISSUE

A good solution to the wrong problem only creates more difficulties. Sometimes we get stuck on a problem, but we are not looking at the real issue. The "Five Whys" process helps you get to the root of a situation. When you are faced with a difficulty, ask yourself why it is a problem. Each time you respond to the question, ask "Why?" again, up to five times. This process will help you explore the deeper reasoning behind what you assume to be the problem. It will force you to evaluate your basic assumptions and reveal gaps in your thinking. Work to find new insights into seemingly unresolvable problems.

39 Ask yourself why you perceive an issue as a problem.

POINTS TO REMEMBER

● Understanding what others are feeling enables you to manage your relationships actively.

● When you have a difficult deadline, you should try and imagine what will happen if you fail to meet it.

● You should examine the real root of a problem, rather than assuming that you know what the issue is.

40 Remember that problems are opportunities for change.

◀ ANALYZING PROBLEMS
This manager has financial problems and wants to increase her salary. Using the "Five Whys" process, she changes the focus of the problem and finds a solution.

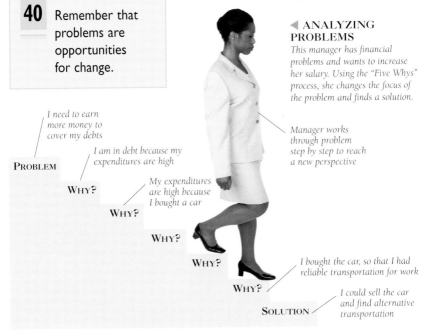

Manager works through problem step by step to reach a new perspective

I need to earn more money to cover my debts

PROBLEM

I am in debt because my expenditures are high

WHY?

My expenditures are high because I bought a car

WHY?

WHY?

WHY?

I bought the car, so that I had reliable transportation for work

WHY?

SOLUTION

I could sell the car and find alternative transportation

CHANGING THE WAY YOU THINK

*In order to be creative, it is necessary
to change the way you think. Learn
to let go of your preconceptions. Understand
the different ways you can reprogram your
mind so that you can see things in different,
more productive ways.*

41 Question and challenge ideas, rather than just accepting them.

THINGS TO DO

1. List and review your main routines.
2. Consider whether these meet your current needs.
3. Make constructive changes to these routines.

DOING THINGS DIFFERENTLY

Telling yourself to "do things differently" is simply an internal prompt that can be used to optimize your personal effectiveness. Notice your usual ways of doing things, such as morning routines, traveling to work routines, job routines, problem-solving routines, relationship-management routines. Analyze these patterns in a creative way and think about how you could change them.

UNFREEZING YOUR MIND

Sometimes your mind freezes and you cannot find a solution to a problem. Disengage from the problem and allow your subconscious mind to work on the issue, undisturbed by the conscious search for a solution. Try going for a walk, thinking about something else, or making a cup of coffee. Use the method that works best for you.

▼ FINDING SOLUTIONS
*Sleeping on a problem can often help.
Go to bed with a problem, leave your
subconscious mind to work at it during
the night, and wake up with the answer.*

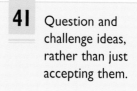

42 Let your subconscious mind find solutions.

DRAWING TO CREATE IDEAS

Many people find visual images are a greater stimulus to creativity than words. Some people find it easier to express themselves by outlining an idea on paper and getting others to comment on what they see. Drawing can also free up your mind to think in a creative way. Get a sheet of paper and draw how you see the solution to a problem. Show it to others and ask them what they see. Use their feedback to help you crystalize your ideas.

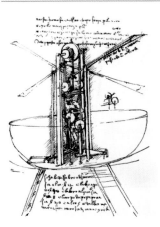

◀ DEVELOPING IDEAS
The Italian Renaissance artist Leonardo da Vinci drew detailed drawings of his many imaginative inventions, such as his ideas for flight.

USING A NEGATIVE CONDITION

Applying a negative condition means creating a situation from which you then have to recover. For example, imagine that your competitor has halved his prices. Having decided on this negative scenario, think of as many ideas as you can for dealing with the situation. Use your creativity to see how you could overcome the problem.

43 Invest time in learning to do things differently, so that you can identify new opportunities.

QUESTIONS TO ASK YOURSELF

Q Could I handle this task differently?

Q In what ways could I improve this process?

Q When did I last make a significant change?

Q Do I feel threatened by new ideas?

Q Am I satisfied with my current routines?

Q Am I willing to make changes?

Imagine that an unforeseen problem has arisen

Think of lots of ideas for combating the situation

Categorize and write your ideas down

Review these ideas to see if they offer any useful insights

Use your insights to identify any current weaknesses

▲ IMAGINING A PROBLEM
Test your creativity and build your confidence in your ability to deal with problems by working through imagined negative scenarios.

USING A CREATIVE APPROACH

There are many ways of applying creativity in your everyday life and many different techniques that can help you do this. Start to use creative thinking in practice.

SELECTING THE APPROACH

Not all situations respond to a creative approach. Some are too simple to warrant the time and effort involved, others need to be reframed first. Understand the decision-making process and how creative thinking techniques can be implemented.

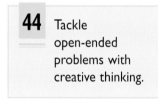

44 Tackle open-ended problems with creative thinking.

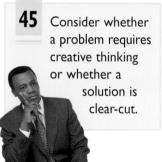

45 Consider whether a problem requires creative thinking or whether a solution is clear-cut.

DECIDING TO BE CREATIVE

The decision to use a creative approach or not depends on the problem. If the problem is simple, for example, you are about to cross a busy road, there is no need to be creative. In fact, being creative could be counterproductive because you need the full power of your logical thinking process to get you safely across the road. However, if you are looking at ways of reducing the number of road fatalities that occur, this is an open-ended problem and a creative approach will offer you more solutions to consider. Recognize the situations where a creative approach would be beneficial.

CATEGORIZING PROBLEMS

Once you have identified that an issue is open-ended, the next step in the process is to categorize it and form a problem statement. Problems can be grouped into three categories: personal, such as an illness; professional, such as a career change opportunity; or they can involve a third party, such as an issue that you want to help someone else to resolve. Having categorized the problem, define it and rephrase it – this will help you look at it in a different way.

PROBLEM STATEMENT ▶

Restating a problem allows you to see it from a different perspective, so that you can find fresh solutions.

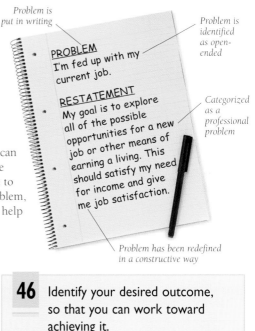

Problem is put in writing

PROBLEM
I'm fed up with my current job.

RESTATEMENT
My goal is to explore all of the possible opportunities for a new job or other means of earning a living. This should satisfy my need for income and give me job satisfaction.

Problem is identified as open-ended

Categorized as a professional problem

Problem has been redefined in a constructive way

UNDERSTANDING CONTEXTS

During the creative process, it is important to identify all the parties who have a stake in the solution of the problem. This is so that the solution matches the needs of everyone involved. For example, at an international level, there is no point looking at the political issues in the Middle East without considering the Western concerns about oil. If this is not taken into account, it is unlikely that a suggested solution will gain agreement.

46 Identify your desired outcome, so that you can work toward achieving it.

VISUALIZING OUTCOMES

Now that you have prepared your problem statement, imagine the outcome that you want to achieve. Visualizing your goal will help you clarify what you want to achieve through the creative process, and it will also help you judge the ideas you generate. Imagine actually achieving your goal. Think about how you will feel – will you feel pleased, relieved, or still uncertain? Your response is an indication of whether you really do want the outcome and it will also help to make your goal very compelling. Think about how well this outcome fits in with your other goals. Does it fit in with the direction you want your life to go in?

CHOOSING THE RIGHT TOOL

When you have clarified the desired outcome, the next step is to select the appropriate creative tool to help you achieve it. Like choosing the right golf club, choosing the right tool is crucial to the success of the creative process. Sometimes you will need to use a combination of tools; for example, you might choose a "mind map" to clarify a problem, and then try "imposing a negative condition" to help you generate ideas. Once you have come up with ideas, use "logical thinking" to analyze them.

47 Use creative tools to help you think in more productive ways.

48 Learn how to select the right tool to achieve the best result.

USING A CREATIVE TOOL▼

Once you have decided that a problem requires a creative approach, choose the appropriate tool and use it to help you find an effective solution.

Identify the open-ended problem to be solved and think about the creative tools you could use	How can I deal with this complex problem?	I could break it up into manageable parts
Select a tool that will help you break the problem down, such as mind mapping	What is the main crux of this problem?	I will focus on this before looking at the side issues
Impose a condition, so that you can view the problem from a different angle	How else could I look at this issue?	I will gain some unexpected insights and ideas
Having generated some ideas, select the best one and start to put it into practice	What action could I now take?	I will form a plan and start to implement it

CHOOSING THE RIGHT TOOL FOR THE PROBLEM

TOOL	PROBLEM TYPE	APPLICATION
MIND MAPPING	Suitable for problems that have many parts, such as buying a house.	Provides a framework for breaking down a complex situation and enabling creative thought.
USING A NEGATIVE CONDITION	For problems where you need to generate creative ideas.	Changes your perspective and helps you generate new ideas on a topic by imagining a negative scenario.
PHYSICAL ACTIVITY	For problems that need quiet reflection, such as communicating bad news.	Frees up your mind for jumping mental hurdles.
THE HELICOPTER APPROACH	Useful when you want to understand what others are really feeling.	Lifts you above your problem, so that you notice nonverbal behavior and respond appropriately in a situation.
IMPOSED CONDITION	Suitable for finding a new paradigm, like managing a life change.	Changes the shape of a problem. Provides a different perspective and allows new ideas to be evaluated.
THE FIVE WHYS	Useful for dealing with problems that have hidden agendas.	Helps you "drill down" into a situation to find the real problem, clarify issues, and form creative solutions.
DOING THINGS DIFFERENTLY	For situations in which you are seeking to make improvements.	Helps you find ways of improving personal effectiveness, and focusing your mind on what could be done differently.
OUTCOME THINKING	Useful when you want to focus on what needs to be achieved.	Enables you to clarify desired outcomes before the start of the problem-solving process.
UNFREEZING	For problems where you cannot think of any more ideas.	Helps you when your thinking process is blocked or shut down and you cannot find any solutions.
DRAWING	For problem solvers who feel happier expressing themselves graphically.	Empowers your ability to express yourself. An essential tool for people who think in a visual way.

APPLYING YOUR CREATIVITY

When you generate creative ideas, it is necessary to check that your ideas meet your needs. Make sure that you are clear about what you want to achieve. Check that your ideas are relevant, and then refine them, so that they are ready to share.

49 Believe there is a better way to do things and then find out what it is.

RECOGNIZING THE NEED

New ideas are born out of the need to change something. Human beings are motivated to satisfy their needs and, when a need is not being met, they search for a solution to resolve this situation. Recognition of a need occurs when you identify your current situation with a preferred alternative and find the latter attractive. Having recognized this need, you are in a position to identify a satisfactory solution.

◀ **IDENTIFYING YOUR NEEDS**
This manager finds that he has to take work home in order to achieve deadlines on a project. He realizes that this causes him stress so he decides to renegotiate his schedules with his superiors.

BEING CREATIVE

It is relatively easy to go out and find a new job when you are dissatisfied with your current one; this is a logical approach. But is it the answer for you? Maybe not. Most people who change jobs are not really any more satisfied than they were before. This is because they did not clarify the need they were really trying to satisfy, and they did not creatively explore the opportunities open to them. Clarify what you really want: for example, more interesting work, more freedom, less routine. Use the "Five Whys" approach and then use an "alternative thinking" approach to generate ideas.

50 Write down your ideas and start to evaluate them.

51 Think about what you would like in an ideal world.

USING REFRAMING

Reframing is a useful way to clarify your needs and help you generate new solutions.
For example, perhaps you are unhappy in your job. Instead of thinking about finding a
new job, start to think about how you could feel more fulfilled at work:

*I would feel more valued if I
were given more responsibility and
had greater challenges.*

*I would enjoy my job more if I
were able to change my working hours
and have more time to myself.*

*I enjoy working with others,
so I should concentrate on
developing team projects.*

*I would find my job more
satisfying if I received feedback from
my boss – I will ask for a review.*

ANALYZING IDEAS

Once the ideas have been produced, they need
to be evaluated. This means applying a logical
process. Identify "must" and "want" criteria.
"Must" criteria are the things that have to be
achieved by the decision. For example, if you were
considering a change of job, a "must" criteria might
be to maintain your income at a certain level. A
"want" could be to earn more money in the long
term. Start to assess your ideas against the criteria.

52 Be clear about
your goals and
ideas when you
explain them
to others.

THE FOUR PS

When you present an idea, start by
outlining your position – provide an
overview of the background to the
situation. Discuss why the situation is
a problem and highlight any quantifiable
data. Outline the possible courses of
action. Mention the advantages and
disadvantages associated with each
possible choice. Put forward your
proposal, and highlight its benefits.

SELLING YOUR IDEAS

All ideas have to be presented to
someone at some stage in the process in
order to gain approval for action. The way
a presentation is made can determine the
success of a proposal. There are varying
ways of structuring a presentation but
one of the best known and most effective
is called the "Four Ps" method. Introduce
your idea and outline your position. Then,
define the problem, detail the possible
courses of action, and put forward your
proposed solutions.

IMPLEMENTING IDEAS

Creativity has value only if it is turned into action. Understand the process by which creative ideas are turned into realistic plans. Make sure that you are able to monitor progress, and always be ready to deal with difficulties should they arise.

53 Recognize that ideas that are left unimplemented have no value.

54 Write out an action plan, so that you can begin to put your ideas into practice.

DEVELOPING A PLAN

Once an idea has been accepted, the next step is to produce an action plan. A formal plan will provide you with a structured and thorough approach. It will also enable you to communicate your ideas to others. List the activities that are required for the implementation of the idea. Prioritize the actions. Estimate the time that each activity will take and produce a plan.

ALLOCATING WORK

When a plan has been agreed upon, the next step is to allocate the tasks. If you are implementing the project alone, do the tasks in the planned order. However, if you are managing a team that will, for example, be developing a new product, then the tasks will need to be delegated. Use the "Prime Model" to help guide your team through a project.

USING THE PRIME MODEL ▶

When you are putting proposals into action, use a structured approach. Make sure that you have all the necessary resources. Then, delegate tasks, monitor progress, and evaluate results.

PREPARATION
Collect the necessary materials

READINESS
Organize your resources

IMPLEMENTATION
Carry out and delegate work

MONITORING
Keep checking progress

EVALUATION
Ensure you achieve the goal

55 Make sure that all your team members are clear about the goals of the project.

MONITORING ACTION

In order for your ideas to be implemented successfully, you need to have the means of comparing actual results against planned outcomes. Make sure you have clear, measurable objectives. "Hard" objectives, such as winning a key account within three months, are easy to measure. A "soft" objective, such as improving your organization's efficiency, is more difficult to measure. However, you might measure it in terms of an increase in production. Assess how you will measure success.

56 See how action plans help you work with others.

REVIEWING PROGRESS ▼

Meet with your project team each week so that you can discuss progress. Work together to find creative ways to deal with unexpected problems.

THINGS TO DO

1. List individual tasks in a logical order.

2. Estimate the time each activity will take and the resources required.

3. Form and brief a team and monitor progress.

MANAGING PROBLEMS

Even in the best-managed projects, problems occur. Think of problems as opportunities to be creative. If, for example, the idea for a new product or service runs into a roadblock, look for an unplanned solution. Anticipate any potential problems and be prepared to deal with them. Keep comparing the current situation against your plan and take the necessary action to correct any deviation, either before or after it occurs.

Coordinator discusses an unexpected problem

Assistant thinks of ideas

Manager notes down any possible solutions

INVOLVING CREATIVE PEOPLE

Sometimes we need to employ people with acknowledged creative talent to help us find the solution to our problems. Recognize the benefits of working with creative specialists, and provide the right environment for them to thrive in.

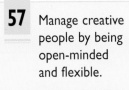

57 Manage creative people by being open-minded and flexible.

WORKING WITH MEN AND WOMEN

It can be beneficial to work with mixed gender teams. This is because women are thought to be more creative than men. They are conditioned to have greater psychological freedom and to think in unconventional ways, whereas men are traditionally conditioned to think logically. This combination of thinking can be very effective.

SEEKING ADVICE ▶
From time to time, we need the help of creative professionals, such as office planners, to help us find new solutions.

58 Evaluate creative ideas before you judge them.

CREATIVE PEOPLE

Some people are naturally creative because they have open minds, intense curiosity, and high levels of energy. They may "see" more than the rest of us. For example, artists can often see colors and shapes in much greater detail than other people can, and they instinctively know how to convey three-dimensional information in one dimension. Recognize the situations where you would benefit from employing a creative person to help you find solutions to complex problems. It is often time and money well spent.

CHOOSING THE RIGHT PEOPLE

The creative professional you choose to seek advice from will depend on the problem you are dealing with. If it is personal, such as you are looking for a new challenge, seek advice from someone who has a lifestyle you would like to emulate. If the problem is professional, such as you are unfulfilled in your current job, consult a recruitment agency. If the problem is organizational, for example, low productivity, invite a consultant with a track record for finding creative solutions to productivity problems to come and present his or her ideas.

59 Avoid rejecting ideas without considering them.

BUILDING A ▶ PICTURE

In this example, a large clothing retailer began to lose its customer base. By recruiting an innovative design team and creating a new range of clothes, the retailer was able to restore its flagging profits.

CASE STUDY

A large clothing retailer found itself in difficulties. Its products and image had become outdated and its traditional customers were deserting it. The end-of-year results were poor.

The organization tried a number of different ways to help improve its disappointing results, including changing its top management and looking for alternative suppliers, but all without success.

The management team then took a close look at what they actually wanted to achieve, so that they had criteria against which to measure success. They wanted to get their results back on track, and to do this they realized they needed to win their customers back. They recruited two new design teams to improve their product. The designers completely remodeled the main product line, and the retailer became profitable again.

60 Always involve positive people in your decisions, as they often produce the best ideas.

MANAGING CREATIVE PEOPLE

Truly creative people tend to see themselves as gifted and in a class of their own. They need a degree of freedom in order to work effectively. Provide them with an informal framework within which to work. Give them clearly defined outcomes for their activities and supply the necessary resources. Involve them at the forefront of the decision-making process.

WORKING WITH OTHERS

Although we all have ideas that we incorporate into our daily lives, it can be difficult to encourage others to follow us. Develop ideas with others and build consensus and commitment.

WORKING TOGETHER

Creativity is stimulated when ideas are shared with others. Recognize that people will be better motivated if they are involved in generating the ideas that lead to decisions. Support others and be ready to show them how to use creative techniques.

61 Remember that collective thinking can reap many successful ideas.

62 Acknowledge that everyone has something to offer.

INVOLVING OTHERS

All ideas need the support of others to become reality. The best way of gaining this support is to discuss your ideas with everyone who will be affected by your decisions. Involve other people in developing new ideas, rather than trying to get them to accept your own ideas. Cooperate with others in order to gain their commitment for agreed upon actions.

GAINING COOPERATION ▼
If people are involved in looking for ideas, they are committed to the task and motivated toward a resolution.

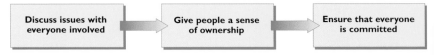

Discuss issues with everyone involved → Give people a sense of ownership → Ensure that everyone is committed

THINGS TO DO

1. Encourage your team to think of ideas.
2. Ask them to put forward as many ideas as possible.
3. Work with them to assess ideas and agree on the actions you will take.

SUPPORTING EACH OTHER

Constructive debate empowers people in a meaningful way. When people all have the same opinion, ideas can stagnate. We need new ideas and these can come only from proactive people who are not afraid to speak up. When everyone else is saying something is not possible, be the person who says, "Why not?" Use creative tools to help optimize the creativity of others and to provide a structure around which you can all generate and then analyze ideas.

UNDERSTANDING TOOLS

Before you use creative tools with a team of people, study the applications of all the tools, and select the best one for your needs. If you have not used the tool before, find someone who has and ask for his or her advice. Get a small group together and organize a practice session before you do the exercise for real.

63 Learn how to use the necessary creative tools.

64 Aim to develop a team's creative potential.

PRACTICING USING A TOOL ▼

In this meeting, a manager is acting as a coach and observing how a team uses a creative tool. At the end of the exercise, the coach reviews how it went and makes suggestions.

Coordinator listens to coach's suggestions

Coach offers feedback

Assistant takes notes for team to refer to after meeting

Sales manager acknowledges points made

SETTING UP TEAMS

The most effective way of capturing your staff's innate creativity is to work in teams. Identify who will be affected by any decisions you make, be ready to bring the best out of other people, and start to put your creative team together.

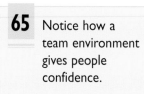

65 Notice how a team environment gives people confidence.

66 Share ideas so that you can fine-tune them.

67 Remember that open debate produces consensus.

GATHERING INPUT

To decide whether you need a team or an individual approach to a problem, ask yourself, "Will I need the commitment of others to implement my solution?" If the answer is "yes," make sure you involve the necessary people in the problem-solving process. For example, a decision to refurbish the office will affect the majority of employees and they will all expect to be consulted. Take everyone's views into account.

▼ INVOLVING OTHERS
This manager asks his staff how they feel about a departmental restructuring. He listens to what each has to say, and he will incorporate their views into his decisions.

Manager asks his team for comments on the restructuring

Team member has comments to make

Takes notes on feedback he receives

LEADING CREATIVE TEAMS

As the team leader, you have the task of taking your team through the process of generating ideas. At "ideas meetings," be ready to adopt a different style of leadership from the one you would normally use at operational meetings. Think about how you will structure the creative meeting and how you will encourage everyone to contribute.

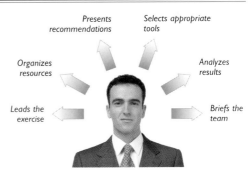

Presents recommendations

Selects appropriate tools

Organizes resources

Analyzes results

Leads the exercise

Briefs the team

▲ A GOOD TEAM LEADER
When you are managing creative teams, make sure that you brief your team well. Show others how to use creative tools and lead creative exercises effectively, so that you get excellent results.

POINTS TO REMEMBER

- The creative process should focus on generating ideas, rather than assessing them.
- The team is responsible for the work and the results – the team leader acts as the guide.
- The joint mental capacity of many people is superior to the brains of a few.

FORMING CREATIVE TEAMS

When you have identified who will be affected by your ideas, start to form your team. The optimum group size for a creative exercise is seven to nine people, so if 100 people will be affected by your decision, choosing a team becomes more difficult. You could repeat the exercise 10 times with 10 separate groups or ask each group of 10 to appoint a representative, and invite these representatives to meet with you.

◄ BRIEFING TEAMS
Just as a soccer coach will brief his team and offer it guidance, make sure that everyone on your creative team is clear about the goals you have set.

68 Make sure the composition of the team is appropriate for the problem.

FACILITATING THE PROCESS

Teams can solve problems on their own, but with a good leader, they will also gain the full benefit of this learning experience. As team leader, make sure that your team is well briefed and create the right conditions for them to generate ideas.

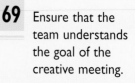

69 Ensure that the team understands the goal of the creative meeting.

ORGANIZING THE PROCESS

Arrange the necessary accommodation for the creative meeting. Choose a large room with comfortable chairs and provide light refreshments. Make sure that there will be no disruptions and remove any telephones. Think through the goals of the meeting. For example, if the problem is a customer complaint, your meeting goal could be to, "Find a solution to the problem and ensure that it does not recur."

BRIEFING THE TEAM

Supply your team with information about the meeting in advance and make sure that they understand the goals of the exercise. For example, the meeting may be taking place to find a solution to a customer satisfaction problem. Outline what creative tool you have chosen to use and make sure that everyone understands how this tool works. State that everyone will have the chance to present their ideas and that these ideas will then be reviewed before a course of action is decided upon.

70 Make sure that you prepare well for your meeting.

Manager sends brief to team via email

SENDING AGENDAS ▶
Before the meeting, email your team a clear agenda so that they know what to prepare for. Explain the process and the goal.

PREPARING TO RUN A CREATIVE SESSION

Ideally, a creative session should last no longer than an hour. During the session, at least 30 minutes should be dedicated to the generation of ideas. To run a successful creative session you will need the following:

● A large room with no telephones or other distractions.

● A flip chart, lots of paper, magic markers, and adhesive tape.

● A "U" shape seating layout around the flip chart.

● A group of people, most of whom should be closely involved with the issue

in question. Ideally, the session should also include two or three people who are "outside" the problem – they will be invaluable for stimulating new ideas and for offering different perspectives on the issues.

● A problem to be addressed, and a clear goal to work toward. This should be written up on the flip chart, so that the focus of the meeting is always in view of everyone. If the meeting veers off its course, you can steer people back to the issue in question by pointing to the flipchart.

LEADING THE EXERCISE

The leader's role is to support the creative process by adopting an open style of leadership. This means providing a structure that frees people from their usual behavior patterns. Encourage less vocal team members to speak up, and challenge unconstructive behavior. Inspire the sharing and the sparking of ideas by asking open questions and discouraging team members from being judgmental. Be neutral about suggestions and value all contributions.

71 Listen carefully, and make notes you can refer to.

CULTURAL DIFFERENCES

In some countries, such as Japan and India, employees have a tendency to follow the lead of their managers, rather than taking the initiative themselves. In Western countries, such as the United States, organizations tend to encourage all their staff to offer their points of view and come up with creative ideas.

DOS AND DON'TS

✔ Do take every suggestion seriously – take ideas to their logical conclusions.

✔ Do help, support, and guide the process of creative thinking.

✘ Don't reject ideas just because they seem drastic or ridiculous.

✘ Don't influence the group by expressing your own ideas and opinions too freely.

BRAINSTORMING

This team technique is ideally suited for solving open problems. It is a simple means of generating a large number of ideas from a group of people in a short space of time. Teams enjoy the process because it is interesting and it makes people feel valued. It helps provide new solutions to old problems – take full advantage of all the ideas that are gathered.

72 Just call ideas out, rather than thinking about them first.

Write the problem down – try stating it in several ways

⬇

Select the best statement of the problem

⬇

Begin to brainstorm about the problem – call for ideas

⬇

Identify the best ideas and brainstorm further

⬇

Categorize ideas and identify instant winners

Assistant puts forward idea

All team members are fully involved

▲ A BRAINSTORMING SESSION
Brainstorming sessions can be run in a number of different ways, but they should always be lively, fun, and informal. The atmosphere should be conducive to spontaneous creativity.

RUNNING THE SESSION

Start a brainstorming session by outlining the task or problem to be worked on. Explain what is expected of everyone and how the process will work. Write the problem on the flip chart. Phrase it in constructive terms, such as, "How can we reduce the production time?" Then, work your way through the brainstorming process.

73 Suspend judgment, encourage the generation of ideas, and let other people's thoughts inspire you.

◀ THE BRAINSTORMING PROCESS
Work through the brainstorming session in a structured way. If ideas are slow in forthcoming, encourage further input. Leave the evaluation of any ideas until the end of the meeting.

USING DATA DUMPING

Data dumping is a highly visual method of producing ideas and it allows group consensus to be formed. The results are also much easier to evaluate than they are in a brainstorming session because the ideas are categorized. Start a data dumping session by stating a problem. Give each participant a set of adhesive note pads and ask them to write down his or her ideas in capital letters, using key words only. Each idea should be written on a separate note. Participants should take turns presenting their ideas while others ask them questions. As the leader, identify common themes and mark them on the flip chart. Tell the participants to put their notes under the appropriate headings – in this way, ideas are categorized. At the end of the session, agree on the action to be taken.

Leader asks assistant to clarify point

Adhesive notes are placed under category headings

Assistant outlines her idea

Team member thinks of an idea in response to what his colleague says

Leader directs session and makes sure team stays focused

FORMING IDEAS ▲
During a data dumping session, make sure that each team member is given the opportunity to explain his or her views.

ANALYZING YOUR IDEAS

Ideas need to be analyzed to make sure that they are workable and meet your specified criteria. After a creative session, evaluate all the ideas against your goals. Identify instant winners, categorize ideas, and decide what could be implemented.

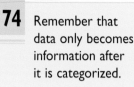

74 Remember that data only becomes information after it is categorized.

75 Pinpoint the ideas that are obviously instant winners.

76 Choose the easiest ideas to implement initially.

RECOGNIZING WINNERS

An instant winner is an idea that can be put in place immediately, providing instant benefits. For example, in a major management attitude change program, the idea was to provide training for 800 managers from five different sites. Conventional training sessions were considered impractical so a brainstorming session was held to find a solution. This produced an idea that was an instant winner: "Train them all at once." The result was a training session held in a local facility capable of holding a large number of people, with successful results.

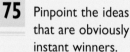

CASE STUDY
Jane was a product manager for a sporting goods company. Products were sold by a sales force through distributors. Jane started to notice that the number of orders she received in some months was very low, while other months showed strong sales.
Jane raised this issue with her managers, and they brainstormed about the problem at the sales conference. The goal was to create more stable sales figures. It then emerged that the real problem was that when the sales people saw they were having a poor month, they made it very poor by moving orders into the following month, thus ensuring their next month's bonus.
One suggestion was that commission should be paid against an annual sales target instead of monthly ones. This idea was put in place and sales began to meet targets.

◀ **IMPLEMENTING YOUR IDEAS**
In this example, a manager noticed that sales figures were fluctuating month to month. The issue was discussed at the sales conference. One of the suggested ideas was implemented and sales figures started to become more consistent.

CATEGORIZING IDEAS

With the exception of brainstorming, categorization is an integral part of the process of all the creative tools. After a brainstorming session, however, you are generally left with a large amount of random information. This then has to be captured and analyzed. The most effective way of doing this is to form categories. Once you have done this, list the ideas under the category headings. Highlight the ideas that are easy to implement and make sure that radical ideas are included in the list.

77 Choose categories that will help you manage the data.

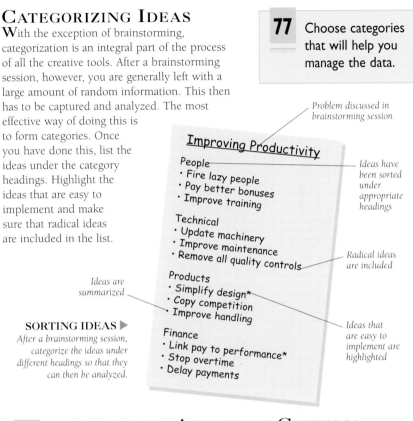

Problem discussed in brainstorming session

Improving Productivity

People
- Fire lazy people
- Pay better bonuses
- Improve training

Technical
- Update machinery
- Improve maintenance
- Remove all quality controls

Products
- Simplify design*
- Copy competition
- Improve handling

Finance
- Link pay to performance*
- Stop overtime
- Delay payments

Ideas have been sorted under appropriate headings

Radical ideas are included

Ideas that are easy to implement are highlighted

Ideas are summarized

SORTING IDEAS ▶
After a brainstorming session, categorize the ideas under different headings so that they can then be analyzed.

78 Judge ideas on their achievability and their value, and rate them on a scale of one to 10.

ASSESSING CRITERIA

Now that you have categorized the ideas, you can begin to rate them. For example, if the brainstorming ideas were focused on improving productivity, judge ideas by considering their impact on performance. Assess all of the ideas against this criterion. Once you have identified the ideas that meet the need, rate them in terms of achievability and value using a 10-point scale. Then, select the ideas you will implement.

STIMULATING IDEAS

People can find generating ideas difficult, especially when it means moving into the unknown. Try to find best practice examples to help inspire your team. Lead people with confidence, and ask questions that open new avenues of thought.

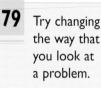

79 Try changing the way that you look at a problem.

Identify an area for improvement

⬇

Select a "best practice" example as a comparison

⬇

Brainstorm the characteristics of the selected best practice

⬇

Compare these characteristics with the area to be improved

⬇

Identify areas that offer opportunities for improvements

⬇

Carry out a detailed assessment and form an action plan

80 Empower people to generate solutions.

MAKING COMPARISONS

Provide your team with a structure for creating "outside-the-box" solutions to existing problems. To help generate and assess ideas, try comparing the features of something you would like to improve against a best practice example. This method is known as Metaphor Analysis. Begin by thinking in general terms about what you want to achieve and then ask yourself, "Where in business, sports, or nature is this already done well?" Then ask, "What are the features that make it successful?" Compare your current situation against the best practice situation, and start to generate ideas.

◀ USING METAPHOR ANALYSIS
This method helps to refresh and stimulate tired minds. It encourages people to break down conventional procedures and move toward a new and more desirable future.

DOS AND DON'TS

✔ Do work through ideas with your team.

✔ Do notice how other organizations deal with similar problems.

✔ Do seek inspiration from different sources, even if the connection seems oblique.

✘ Don't force ideas if you are not in the mood.

✘ Don't reject comparisons without giving them due consideration.

✘ Don't assume that there is only one right answer.

BEING ASSERTIVE

Our interpersonal behavior can be characterized as either directive, passive, or assertive. Directive behavior, which involves telling people how to do things, is designed to get things done in the way we would like. Passive behavior is the acceptance of someone else's directions. Assertive behavior is based on questioning what we do, as well as seeing new and better ways of doing things. Be assertive when you lead others, so that you open the door for suggestions and ideas.

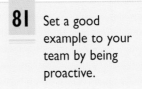

81 Set a good example to your team by being proactive.

▼ ASSESSING BEHAVIOR
Passive behavior is fine in an unchanging world, but assertive behavior holds the key to the future.

BEING PASSIVE | BEING ASSERTIVE

What is the procedure I should follow?

How have you tackled this in the past?

What would you do if you were me?

Why do we follow these procedures?

How could we approach this differently?

Let's look at the options open to us here

82 Use questions that challenge accepted thought.

83 Use closed questions to access information.

ASKING QUESTIONS

There are two types of question: open-ended questions – those that seek general information while also generating dialogue; and closed questions – those that ask for specific information and discourage discussion. Open-ended questions are those that cannot be answered with a straight "yes" or "no" response. Recognize that these types of question are the lifeblood of creativity. Use open-ended questions to encourage your team to think creatively and explore ideas. Help them "get outside the box" of accepted thought.

BEING SPECIFIC

Sometimes it is useful to use closed questions, for instance when you want to find out some specific information. There are two main types of closed question. There are those that produce definite "yes" and "no" answers, such as questions that begin with, "Did you...?," "Can you...?," "Will you...?" And there are those that seek specific answers and facts, such as, "How old are you?" or, "What is your name?" – these provide reference information. Once something specific has been identified, explore it by using open questions.

RESEARCHING DATA ▶
Closed questions can be used to find specific answers in surveys, such as market research questionnaires.

---

84 Be polite when you ask people questions.

QUESTIONS TO ASK YOUR TEAM

Q How do you think we should deal with this?

Q What do you think could be done to improve the current situation?

Q Why do you believe that it is not possible to change things?

Q How do you think it would be possible to benchmark our performance?

Q What would you do if you were in charge?

USING OPEN-ENDED QUESTIONS

Open-ended questions result in answers that give you clues about the other person's feelings. Such questions might be, "What do you hope to do when you have finished college?" or, "What did you think about that film?" The answers provide a broader response, as well as an insight into the attitude of the respondent. The easiest way to ask an open-ended question is to begin with a request such as, "Please outline your views on..." or, "Please tell me a little about..." Use phrases that indicate that you want to hear an opinion.

---

85 Use closed questions to start a discussion, and then develop it by asking open questions.

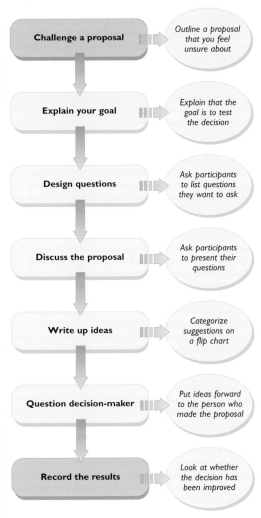

Challenge a proposal	→	Outline a proposal that you feel unsure about
Explain your goal	→	Explain that the goal is to test the decision
Design questions	→	Ask participants to list questions they want to ask
Discuss the proposal	→	Ask participants to present their questions
Write up ideas	→	Categorize suggestions on a flip chart
Question decision-maker	→	Put ideas forward to the person who made the proposal
Record the results	→	Look at whether the decision has been improved

▲ ASKING QUESTIONS

This questioning process is used to help you challenge a proposal. It is a valuable way of adapting ideas, but it should be carried out tactfully in order to achieve the best results.

EXAMINING IDEAS

Use a process to help you challenge your own or other people's ideas. In this way, you can test proposals and pinpoint possible improvements. Bear in mind that people can feel threatened when their ideas are scrutinized and that they may take criticisms personally. Be diplomatic, or your questions will be counter productive. If you have suggestions to make, use examples from another unrelated situation. Be ready to listen to feedback and to learn from other people.

POINTS TO REMEMBER

- When pressed to make changes, some people may harden their position.
- Sometimes it is necessary to push for change gently.
- Change means letting go of the past in order to embrace the challenges of the future.

86 Be sensitive when asking questions – avoid making people feel as if they are being interrogated.

REVIEWING IDEAS

O rganizations waste a great deal of money every year on new ideas that fail because they have not been challenged and examined objectively. Use the different perspectives of your team members to test the potential of ideas.

87 Challenge ideas to make sure you understand what they represent.

88 Decide whether you are a dreamer, a realist, or a critic.

89 Notice what roles people in your team tend to play.

EMPLOYING A STRATEGY

The Disney Strategy is based on a method that Walt Disney used to solve problems. His philosophy was to integrate creative and logical thinking so that they took place in a sequence. In this way, ideas could be properly examined and problems effectively solved. He said that every meeting should have a "dreamer," a "realist," and a "critic" present. Each of these types of thinkers has an important role to play in the examination of ideas. Identify what kind of thinker you and other members of your team are.

RECOGNIZING DIFFERENT TYPES OF THINKERS

THE DREAMER
This is the role of a person who is not bound by convention or restricted by tradition. This person is excellent at coming up with visionary ideas for his or her organization.

THE REALIST
This person takes a concept and asks questions like, "How would this work?" He or she approaches plans in a practical way. Sometimes he or she takes action before all the outcomes have been assessed.

THE CRITIC
This person thinks logically. He or she can see the vision, accept the workable details, and can also see the pitfalls. The critic can be overcautious, but he or she makes sure that the realist's plans are feasible.

- An objective is something you want to achieve, and a strategy is how you plan to realize it.
- When you choose to play a role, do it with conviction.
- Ideas can be accepted only if they are openly challenged and openly defended.
- You can eliminate risks if you take the time to research the situation first.

USING DISNEY STRATEGY

Bring together a team of people and ask for volunteers to be the dreamer, the realist, and the critic. Present the group with a problem to be solved and give them 10 minutes to think about it. Let the dreamer present ideas, ask the realist to consider plans, and let the critic identify the possible pitfalls. At the end, review the results.

▼ LISTENING TO DIFFERENT THINKERS

Different types of thinker can give varying perspectives on an old problem – there is room for a dreamer, a realist, and a critic on every creative thinking team.

Ask the dreamer to come up with ideas	Let the realist analyze the possibilities	Allow the critic to find potential problems

USING ROUNDS

One of the major problems with working in a team is that it can be easy for the powerful to dominate the weak. Using "rounds" enables the leader to manage the group in a democratic way, so that the weak can be as powerful as the strong. Any participant can stop the discussion and ask for a round. Each participant must then state his or her view on the subject, without fear of being interrupted.

90 Make sure that everyone has the chance to speak.

Sales assistant has her say

Leader sets example by listening to each team member

CALLING FOR A ROUND ▶

In this example, the sales assistant asks for a "round" and states her view. Each person then gives his or her view on the issue.

IMPROVING YOUR PROCEDURES

For organizations to remain competitive, they need continually to develop what they do and the way that they do it. Apply creative methods to analyze procedures and review your organization's practices to make sure that they are efficient and up-to-date.

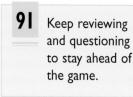

91 Keep reviewing and questioning to stay ahead of the game.

92 Analyze your current procedures to see how they can be improved.

REVIEWING PROCESSES

The profitability of organizations is determined by the effectiveness with which they convert customer orders into goods and services. This "conversion" is achieved though a series of inter-related operational processes. These determine how effectively things get done. Process re-engineering is a method of assessing procedures and adjusting them if necessary. Use it to review and update your organizational processes.

REVIEWING VALUE

Organizations that wish to remain competitive must regularly review their products, processes, and materials. Value reengineering is used to reinvent or update the products organizations make or the services they deliver. The goal is to ensure that all products and services are subjected to regular reviews to assess how they can be improved in the light of new technology, new materials, and new methods. For example, it may be possible to substitute new plastic materials for the metal parts used in a product, or it could be more cost-effective to subcontract a process rather than carrying it out "in-house."

CULTURAL DIFFERENCES

Optimizing the value of an organization means aligning the values of everyone involved – such as managers, employees, suppliers, and customers. The Japanese achieve this by holding reviews. In the United States, market research surveys are put in place to gain feedback on goods and services.

USING TOOLS TO REVIEW PROCESSES AND VALUES

TOOL	STAGES	ACTION
PROCESS REENGINEERING	1. Select the process.	Choose a process you want to review.
	2. Choose your team.	Involve people from all departments.
	3. Outline the process.	Produce a map of the current process.
	4. Identify issues for review.	Look at flaws, blockages, or gaps.
	5. Outline a desired goal.	Show the process as it should be.
	6. Make recommendations.	Explain how to implement ideas.
	7. Monitor action.	Put in place monitoring procedures.
VALUE REENGINEERING	1. Choose the product.	Review all products regularly.
	2. Select the team.	Involve a cross-section of people.
	3. Discuss the product.	Decide on the aspect to be reviewed.
	4. Provide information.	Ensure that product data is available.
	5. Review.	Look at ways of improving the product.
	6. Agree on changes.	Analyze and decide on changes.
	7. Make recommendations.	Outline necessary improvements.

EVALUATING RESULTS

Good proposals need to be refined to make sure that they will do the job they were designed to do. There will always be people who oppose creative solutions, so identify the strengths and weaknesses of your ideas and then present your proposals with confidence.

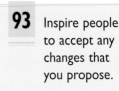

93 Inspire people to accept any changes that you propose.

94 Recognize that poor presentation skills kill ideas.

95 Ask your team to offer ideas on how processes can be improved.

SELECTING PROPOSALS

All creative exercises produce multiple ideas that need to be "waste weeded" and then further refined to enable objective choices to be made. The ranking and rating method is a very effective way of doing this. It can be carried out either by individuals – the resultant data is then analyzed to reach a consensus – or by a team. Start with a list of alternatives. Ask your team to rank each idea in order of preference from one to 10. Then, ask them to rate ideas from one to five, to reflect how effective they believe the chosen solution will be. Record individual rankings and produce a list showing the most valued ideas.

EXAMINING A PROPOSAL

When you are discussing ideas with your team, ask questions that will help develop potentially good ideas further and also find out if there are any potential causes for concern. Here are some examples of things you could say:

Imagine that this change has been put in place. How will it affect our customers?

If we took this idea a step further, what other implications would there be?

If this idea is so good, what is preventing us from putting it in place immediately?

How could we suggest this change in procedure to our suppliers and distributors?

ANALYZING CHOICES

The tool most commonly used to analyze choices is the SWOT Analysis. The process, usually carried out by a small group, is to analyze a decision in order to identify its Strengths, Weaknesses, Opportunities, and Threats. Analyze the strengths of a proposal. What benefits will it bring? Assess the weaknesses. Could there be potential problems? Will we need new investment? Identify the opportunities. What markets will it open? Examine the threats. Is there a risk that we will lose our existing customers?

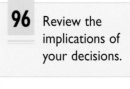

96 Review the implications of your decisions.

97 Consider your ideas from every possible angle.

THINGS TO DO

1. Define your proposition – state what you want to do.

2. Identify positive and negative factors.

3. Use ranking and rating to see which forces will have the greatest impact.

4. Develop an implementation plan that builds on the positive forces and minimizes the negative.

98 Be convincing when you present your ideas.

PRESENTING IDEAS ▶

Once you are confident in your ideas, present them, explain the benefits, and outline how you can deal with problems.

ASSESSING PROS AND CONS

Force field analysis is a technique for identifying the elements that will help or hinder a proposal. If, for example, you want to introduce an annual review system, you will need to recognize who will actively support the process and who may be against it. For example, employees may approve of review sessions because it will make them feel valued. However, some managers may see reviews as time-consuming and pointless. After these factors have been considered, develop a plan to harness the positive support and reduce the impact of resistance. In this way, you can increase your chances of success.

IMPROVING TEAM EFFECTIVENESS

We can improve the way we work only by reflecting objectively on our performance, identifying the areas for improvement, and than taking action. Aim to improve your own creative performance and that of your team continually.

99 Remember that a team is only as strong as its leader.

100 Use feedback to help improve your skills.

101 Avoid taking criticism personally.

DEVELOPING SKILLS

It is always worthwhile investing in your own skills and personal development, as well as those of your team members. At the end of each project, hold a review and look at how you could have worked more creatively. Notice areas where you could have achieved better results if you had had the necessary know-how, such as technical training or better people-management skills. Keep up to date with developments within your industry, and make trade journals available to your team members, too.

ANALYZING PROJECTS ▼
Review projects with your team and discuss how you could have dealt with issues differently.

Assistant suggests change in procedure

Colleague agrees with assistant

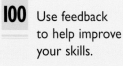

REVIEWING PERFORMANCE

At the end of a project, assemble your team and say that you would like some feedback on your performance. Prepare a questionnaire and distribute it. Ask all team members to complete the form and fill one in yourself. Then, note the key questions on a flip chart and ask participants to say how you scored. Seek explanations for the grading. After the meeting, consider the feedback you received and compare it with your own views on your performance. Identify areas for improvement and decide on actions you will take.

QUESTIONS TO ASK YOURSELF

Q Did I run that project well, or did I tend to seek quick solutions, instead of taking the time to think creatively?

Q What areas of my performance do I need to improve?

Q Have I noticed failings in others that I can also see in myself?

Q Does my analysis of my performance match the views of my team?

▼ ASSESSING YOUR PERFORMANCE

After a creative session, for example a brainstorming exercise, prepare a questionnaire and ask your team to give you feedback on your performance as a leader.

Questionnaire is typed up

Clarifies whether goals were clear

Checks feedback on presentation of ideas

Asks team for their thoughts on time management

Assessment

● Were the objectives of the session well presented and measurable?

● Was the creative process clearly explained?

● Was the session well structured?

● Were topics clearly introduced and debated?

● Did everyone have the opportunity to express new ideas?

● Was creativity encouraged?

● Did all team members feel that their views were valued and appreciated?

● How effective was the team leader at controlling the session?

● Was time managed well?

● Were topics effectively summarized and decisions recorded?

Checks whether team were clear about tools

Gives team members chance to say whether they felt included

Asks for feedback on performance as team leader

ASSESSING YOUR CREATIVITY

Evaluate your current levels of creativity by reading the following statements, and then choosing the option that is closest to your experience. If your answer is "never," circle option 1; if it is "always," circle option 4, and so on. Be honest with yourself. Add your scores together and refer to the analysis to see how you scored. Use your answers to identify areas that need improvement.

OPTIONS

1 Never

2 Occasionally

3 Frequently

4 Always

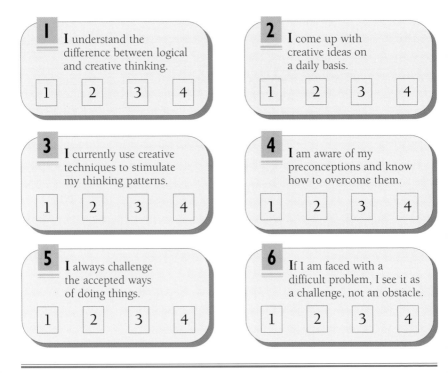

1 I understand the difference between logical and creative thinking.

1 2 3 4

2 I come up with creative ideas on a daily basis.

1 2 3 4

3 I currently use creative techniques to stimulate my thinking patterns.

1 2 3 4

4 I am aware of my preconceptions and know how to overcome them.

1 2 3 4

5 I always challenge the accepted ways of doing things.

1 2 3 4

6 If I am faced with a difficult problem, I see it as a challenge, not an obstacle.

1 2 3 4

7 I believe that I am able to think outside the box of convention.

| 1 | 2 | 3 | 4 |

8 I am good at searching my mind for new solutions to old problems.

| 1 | 2 | 3 | 4 |

9 I often wake up in the morning with new solutions to problems I face.

| 1 | 2 | 3 | 4 |

10 I always make the time to think creatively before analyzing ideas logically.

| 1 | 2 | 3 | 4 |

11 I review processes and procedures regularly, rather than just accepting them.

| 1 | 2 | 3 | 4 |

12 I believe that the impossible is possible if I want it badly enough.

| 1 | 2 | 3 | 4 |

13 I am not ashamed to suggest ideas, even if others may see them as foolish.

| 1 | 2 | 3 | 4 |

14 I regularly question my assumptions to ensure that I am being realistic.

| 1 | 2 | 3 | 4 |

15 I am always willing to listen to someone else's ideas.

| 1 | 2 | 3 | 4 |

16 I always take opportunities to do new things.

| 1 | 2 | 3 | 4 |

17 I accept that others may have difficulty with new ideas and adapt accordingly.

1   2   3   4

18 I regularly visualize my goals, and I find this helps me to solve problems.

1   2   3   4

19 I can see, hear, and feel my world and am happy with my position in it.

1   2   3   4

20 I question decisions if I think that this will lead to better results.

1   2   3   4

21 I sometimes find that people around me find my ideas threatening.

1   2   3   4

22 I keep looking for new ideas, even when I have found a potential solution.

1   2   3   4

23 I understand the value of using creative tools to solve problems.

1   2   3   4

24 I believe that even good habits can be a barrier to creativity.

1   2   3   4

25 I try to adopt a different way of doing something every week.

1   2   3   4

26 I believe that it is necessary to adapt in order to survive.

1   2   3   4

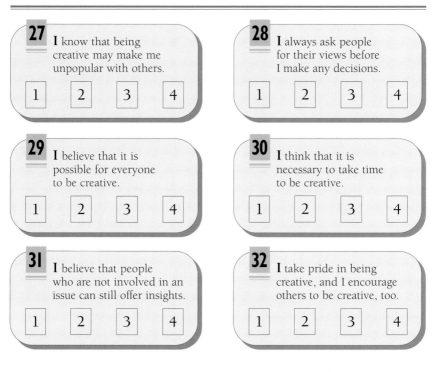

27 I know that being creative may make me unpopular with others.

1   2   3   4

28 I always ask people for their views before I make any decisions.

1   2   3   4

29 I believe that it is possible for everyone to be creative.

1   2   3   4

30 I think that it is necessary to take time to be creative.

1   2   3   4

31 I believe that people who are not involved in an issue can still offer insights.

1   2   3   4

32 I take pride in being creative, and I encourage others to be creative, too.

1   2   3   4

ANALYSIS

Now that you have completed the self-assessment, add up the scores and check your performance by referring to the evaluation below. Identify your weakest areas, and refer to the relevant sections in this book to hone your creativity skills.

32–64: There are many areas of your creativity that you need to work on. Concentrate on changing your preconceptions and set time aside to think more creatively.

64–95: You have a good grasp of how to be creative, but you need to improve your skills further.

96–128: You are well versed in the use of creative techniques and are fully equipped to get the best from your team, too. However, there is always room for improvement.

INDEX